AFFILAT MARKETING

BOOK DESCRIPTION

Affiliate marketing is a multi-billion dollar enterprise. In US alone, Affiliate Marketing is worth almost $7 billion and continues to experience a double digit compound growth. This is such a huge pie that is waiting for you to take a bite. This book is just about that – helping you get a sizeable bite of this pie by relying on your blogging to generate passive income thus turning your hobby into a full-time business – of biting the pie.

Despite Affiliate Marketing having existed for several decades, many people are yet to fathom what it is all about. This books starts off by introducing you to the basics of Affiliate Marketing so that you are well-grounded for a solid take-off.

Biting the pie becomes appetizing when you know what it is in the bite that you are going to gain. This guide recognizes this by showing you the great 'nutritional' benefits that you can derive taking a share of this giant pie – Affiliate Marketing.

The pie doesn't ready itself on your table. You have to know how to get it and bring it onto your dinning table. This book provides you with information on how to get started with Affiliate Marketing with a hands-on practical step-by-step approach so that you can start off as an expert.

Not all utensils are the same when it comes to preparing your pie for a bite. Some are better than others, yet, some are simply different. This too happens when it comes to Affiliate Marketing Platforms (the kind of utensils you need to get a bite of that Affiliate Marketing pie). You too should know how to handle the fork, the knife and other important skills that go along with proper dinning etiquette. The book provides all information you need to get the best Affiliate Marketing platform to turn your hobby into full-time business for a great passive income.

In any marketing endeavor (Affiliate Marketing included), finding the right products to market becomes the key to your success. The product must be capable of selling enough to meet your income needs. Here in this guide, we provide you step-by-step instructions on how to find products to market so that you can quickly and easily optimize on your passive income.

The importance of communication to your marketing endeavor needs not be overemphasized. Communication is crucial. When it comes to online marketing, (more so, Affiliate Marketing), use of email marketing and blogging become the core part of your communication. They are the tools you need, not only to communicate, but also to build audience. The bigger your audience is, the higher is your potential to have a bigger bite of the Affiliate Marketing pie. This guide provides information, tips and strategies on how you can successfully use email marketing and blogging to build a full-time business and optimize on your passive income by leveraging the benefits of a big audience.

You need to generate traffic to your blog in order to build a bigger audience. You need to employ different strategies and tools to enable you to succeed in this. In this guide, we provide you with other ways to attract traffic to your blog beside email marketing. This helps you to advantage of web technology to build bigger audience.

Lastly, there is a limit as to how much donkey work pays. You can't soar high if you work like a donkey. Be smart. Automate your Affiliate Marketing income. This is what builds wealth. You may start by working for money but, the end game is where money starts working for you. This guide provides information on all you need to optimize your business for automated passive income flows.

ABOUT THE AUTHOR

George Pain is an entrepreneur, author and business consultant. He specializes in setting up online businesses from scratch, investment income strategies and global mobility solutions. He has built several businesses from the ground up, and is excited to share his knowledge with readers.

DISCLAIMER

Contents

AFFILATE MARKETING 1

BOOK DESCRIPTION 2

ABOUT THE AUTHOR 5

DISCLAIMER 6

INTRODUCTION 9

WHAT IS AFFILIATE MARKETING? 11

BENEFITS OF AFFILIATE MARKETING 21

GETTING STARTED WITH AFFILIATE MARKETING 24

WHICH ARE THE BEST AFFILATE MARKETING PLATFORMS? 35

HOW TO FIND PRODUCTS TO MARKET 41

USING EMAIL MARKETING 55

USING YOUR BLOG TO MARKET YOUR PRODUCT 61

OTHER WAYS TO ATTRACT TRAFFIC 80

HOW TO AUTOMATE YOUR AFFILIATE MARKETING
INCOME 85

CONCLUSION 92

INTRODUCTION

One of the greatest revolutions brought about by the internet is the freedom to work and earn remotely. The internet, through ecommerce, has also revolutionized the way people shop. Both work and shopping environments have been greatly transformed by the internet. In US alone, it is estimated that 25% of workforce is carrying out its tasks remotely. The rise of Amazon, among other online marketplaces has seen big traditional brick-and-mortar shops downsize and cut down on their future forecasts. You must become part of this revolution to stay afloat or else sink like a stone.

The emergence of blogs and social media has become one of the most disruptive technologies in the publishing industry. This has led to small publishers biting big into market share of traditional giant publishers. The end result has been that big print media continue bleed and shrink. The future is bright for bloggers, especially those who leverage email marketing with social media marketing to monetize their blog. You too can turn your hobby into full-time business for a great passive income.

This guide, Affiliate Marketing, is geared towards equipping you with relevant information and skills that you need to use blogging and affiliate marketing to generate passive income online and turn your hobby into a full-time business.

The practical hands-on information accompanied by step-by-step instructions and great tips will enable you to build a full-time business and optimize on your passive income while enjoying what you love doing – blogging about your hobby.

This book brings you closer to making a giant bite of the multi-billion dollar Affiliate Marketing industry that continues to experience double-digit compound growth. Be part of this great transformation. Be successful.

Keep reading!

WHAT IS AFFILIATE MARKETING?

Affiliate marketing is a kind of marketing system whereby one party (affiliate/publisher) promotes a product of another party (merchant/product creator) through an intermediary (affiliate network/platform) for a reward.

Parties of Affiliate marketing

Affiliate marketing transaction involves the following key parties;

1. **Product Merchant** – Also known as the Product Creator/Product owner, a product merchant is the owner of the product that needs to be promoted.

2. **Affiliate Network Platform** – This is a platform that provides tools, links and analytics for products being promoted. The Affiliate Network acts as a link between the product merchant and the affiliate marketer.

3. **Affiliate Merchant** – This is a business entity that dedicates itself to promoting products, traffic and brand awareness through a network of affiliate sites. As such, they create various kinds of ads including text links ads, static banner ads, flash banners ads, video ads and

sometimes a combination of some them to be placed on affiliate websites. To achieve this, an Affiliate merchant uses an Affiliate network platform.

4. **Affiliate Marketer** (Affiliate/Publisher) – this is the owner of an affiliate website on which affiliate merchant's ads and links are placed. The affiliate marketer endeavors to promote the product to the target audience through content (such as articles, product reviews, how-to instructions, product comparisons, etc).

5. **Consumer (Customer/Buyer)** – this is the person who accesses the product being promoted by an Affiliate via affiliate links and successfully buys the product

Most of the time, affiliate merchants have their own in-house platform. However, in some cases, Affiliate merchants hire an external Affiliate network platform. Thus, it is not uncommon for Affiliate network platform and Affiliate Merchant to be treated one and the same. But, technically, they are not one and the same.

In this book, we will use Affiliate Network Platform and Affiliate Merchant interchangeably. In some instances, we will use Affiliate Network Provider to refer to a combination of both. Nonetheless, it must be noted that an Affiliate Merchant can't work without an Affiliate Network Platform. Thus, whenever

Affiliate Merchant is mentioned, Affiliate Network Platform is implied and vice versa.

How Affiliate Marketing Works

The following steps provide a glimpse of how Affiliate marketing works;

1. A merchant approaches an Affiliate network provider to be helped to promote his/her product
2. Both the Affiliate merchant and the network provider agree on their respective earnings. They also agree on what to pay Affiliates.
3. The network provider creates product-specific link generation system that automatically generates links based on the product merchant's details (product name details) and Affiliate Marketer's details (Affiiate ID)
4. The Affiliate Marketer approaches the Network Provider, gets registered and provided with auto-generated links based on his/her registration details to place on his site/blog
5. The Affiliate Marketer hyperlinks certain parts of the content/space using provided link

6. The Affiliate publishes his/her content on the blog which attracts attention of readers

7. The reader goes through the content, and, if convinced of the need to buy the product being promoted, decides to click on the Affiliate hyperlink.

8. Once the reader (potential buyer) clicks on the hyperlink he/she is redirect to the product's page of the product merchant.

9. If the customer decides to buy the product, this becomes a successful sale through the Affiliate's marketing effort. The details of the purchase are recorded both by the Affiliate Network and the product merchant.

10. On successful sale, the Affiliate's account is credited with the amount due. How soon that is done depends on the security period. Most Affiliate networks provide a security period of less than 30 days. The security period ensures that the Affiliate is not paid yet the customer returns the product later on to claim refund. The security period depends on the product merchant's return policy plus the waiting period added on by the Affiliate Network.

Common terminology that you ought to be aware of

Affiliates – These are the owners of affiliate sites.

Affiliate sites – These are the websites by affiliates where product links and ads are placed and promoted.

Affiliate marketplace – These are central databases for various affiliate programs. Such marketplaces include Commission Junction (CJ), Clickbank and ShareAsale.

Affiliate software – These are special software used by product merchants or affiliate merchants/networks to create affiliate programs. Such software include iDevafilliate.

Affiliate link – this is a special link produced by affiliate software that is provided to you by Affiliate merchant so as to track the progress of your affiliate program. This is the link that you will encourage your readers to click on so as to get access to the product being promoted. It is also the link for all other affiliate ads. You have to ensure that you use this link otherwise you will lose on your commission as the network platform won't be able to register and track your effort.

Affiliate ID – this is an ID that uniquely identifies you and the product being promoted. It is typically embedded into the Affiliate link and Affiliate ads.

Payment mode – this refers to the manner in which you can be paid. Most common payment mode is via direct bank transfer, others include check, PayPal, Skrill, among others. It is important to ascertain whether payment modes offered by the Affiliate merchant are such that they can enable you to receive payment. If not, then, don't pain yourself working for what you cannot receive.

Two-tier affiliate marketing – this is a kind of being a 'double affiliate'. In this case, you not only market products through an affiliate marketplace/platform but also market that platform. For example, you can market products available at Commission Junction. Yet, you can also market Commission Junction itself by encouraging people to join it as affiliate marketers. It is a concept similar to Multi-Level Marketing (MLM).

Link cloaking – Link cloaking simply refers to beautifying an ugly link so that it can become appealing since it is easy to scan and much easier to master. It also involves safeguarding your link against hacking.

Custom coupons – Custom coupons are those kinds of coupons branded by affiliate marketers. They are offered by the product merchant to the affiliate to customize as per the target audience. This helps to build loyalty and trust as the audience can feel that you have some special pricing power or bargain offer that they cannot get elsewhere. Not all product merchants or affiliate platforms offer this facility. You need to be conscious about this as one of the criteria for choosing the right product and platform.

Landing page – A landing page is a special page built solely for the purpose of a single conversion. Thus, ideally, each product must have its own landing page. Though, a product can have multiple landing pages (probably for special discounts, special offers, specific audience, etc). The most common type of landing pages are the subscription forms that pop up immediately or a page opens while scrolling towards the page's downward end. However, any page that is specifically created for purposes of a single conversion is a landing page, be it a pop-up page or not.

Gravity index – refers to how many successful affiliates are promoting a certain given product. For example, if there are 7 affiliates successfully promoting a product, its gravity index will be 7. On the other hand, if there are only 2 affiliates successfully promoting a certain other product, its gravity index will be 2. Thus, the higher the gravity index, the higher is the number of affiliates actively and successfully promoting that particular product. It must be noted that gravity index is not based on volume of products sold but the number of affiliates successfully selling it.

How to earn from Affiliate marketing

Earnings from Affiliate marketing are based on two methods;

- Revenue share
- Commission

Revenue share

This is an earning mode whereby the Affiliate earns a certain percentage of revenue generated from his/her affiliate marketing endeavors. Typical revenue share percentage for the Affiliate marketer can range between 5% and 40% depending on the nature of the product being marketed and the reputation of each of the parties involved.

Commission

This is by far the commonest mode of earning. The Affiliate and the Network provider agree on an affiliate commission to be paid to the Affiliate for his/her promotional endeavors. Typical commissions range from 1% to 40% depending on the nature of product and the reputation of the Parties involved.

Factors determining your earning potential

The greatest thing about Affiliate marketing is that it is highly flexible and unlimited. You determine how much to earn and from which source/network. There are no lower or upper ceilings, although, the ceilings can affect your cash flow.

Your earning depends on several factors. The following are the main factors determining your earning potential;

- Your resourcefulness – Whether traditional or digital, marketing is always a creative endeavor. In traditional marketing, being street-smart is always a plus. In the online marketing, being digital-wise is always a plus. Nonetheless, whichever marketing endeavor, mastering the product you are promoting, reading customer psychology to device an appropriate approach, predicting customer concerns and queries and addressing them in advance, persuasion and art of closing deal are all important.

- Your effort – Hard work pays. Every effort has a unique way of paying you. What is important is to monetize that effort. Don't dwell on efforts that you can't monetize.

- Your focus – it is commonly said that time is money. Much more important, attention is wealth. Where attention is focused is where wealth comes from. You have to focus your effort to wealth generation endeavors. Some efforts may not result in quick cash, thus making one think that they are not monetizeable. However, they can help one create wealth which boosts long-term income potential. For example, you can focus on creating quality blog posts over time. One blog post may not yield much in terms of monetization, but a series of quality expert blog posts in a certain niche can create a loyal following. This loyal following can result in stable long-term income streams.

- Optimization- Whatever you do, seek to optimize it. One of the best ways of optimizing your earning potential is to automate your income streams.

BENEFITS OF AFFILIATE MARKETING

Affiliate marketing is one of the most preferred ways of marketing products by merchants and earning income by publishers. This is due to the immense benefits that accrue to both parties. The network provider comes in to interconnect these benefits so that at the end of it, the consumer gets the product deserved.

Each of the parties to affiliate marketing has unique benefits.

Benefits of Affiliate marketing to the product merchant

1. The product merchant only pays for result, not performance. This means that the product themselves (the revenue) pays for the marketing cost as opposed to the working capital.
2. Products are not just advertised but explained in detail by the publisher. Publishers, being third parties, have a unique and vantage position to properly explain the product features and benefits to the target audience.
3. The process is automated. The product merchant doesn't have to bother much about how the product is being

marketed, how marketers are paid and tracking of each marketer's results. This is done by the network platform. It is up to the network platform to recruit and engage affiliate marketers.

4. Extra exposure
5. Increased SEO ranking

Benefits of Affiliate marketing to the Affiliate merchants/network platform

1. Increased income sources
2. Improved service to customers (product merchants)

To the final Consumer

1. Great information about product
2. Opportunity to seek explanation about product features and how to use
3. Ease of access to the product page

To the Affiliate Marketer

- Multiple income streams
- Passive income
- Incentive to building an audience which can develop into long-term beneficial relationship
- Low investment
- Little operating cost

- 24/7 income flows
- Global marketplace at your fingertips
- Little risks involved
- Own boss
- You can work from anywhere, anytime
- You don't bear the challenges of dealing with customers. E.g. customer complaints, customer attention, etc
- You are in charge of your earning potential

GETTING STARTED WITH AFFILIATE MARKETING

Affiliate marketing is one of the easiest businesses to get started in. This is because;

- It requires very little capital
- There are plenty of affiliate merchants/platforms ready to get new affiliates
- Plenty of products to market

To get started, the following are important steps;

1. Know what Affiliate marketing is all about (see previous section on "what is Affiliate Marketing")
2. Know what is in store for you
3. Decide on your product niche
4. Setup a niche blog/website
5. Find the appropriate affiliate merchant/platform (see next section on "which are the best affiliate marketing platforms?")
6. Get affiliate links of the products you are going to market
7. Cloak your affiliate link
8. Write blog posts relevant to your affiliate product and hyperlink the content to the affiliate links

9. Create a landing page
10. Device appropriate marketing strategies
11. Use email marketing to drive traffic
12. Automate your affiliate marketing income

Know what is in store for you

The 2017 facts about affiliate industry are that;

- Change in search engine algorithm is geared towards favoring high quality organic content (not spun or copied articles). Google punishes you for copying or spinning content.

- Quality content will continue to fuel SEO into the future

- Influencers will continue to lead the affiliate marketing segment

- Over 80% of brands in the developed world utilize affiliate marketing

- More than 50% of affiliate marketing traffic will be derived from mobile phones by year 2020

- About 48% of online users have installed ad blockers which prevent ads from appearing while they are browsing. This has resulted into product merchants to increasingly shift their attention away from PPC (Pay per Click) adverts towards affiliate marketing.

- Ecommerce sales are projected to reach $700 billion by year 2020.

These facts simply mean that;

Your blog is going to be the preferred way of affiliate marketing heading into the future. The era of keyword stuffing, black-hat tricks is increasing getting behind us.

Choosing a niche which you are passionate and knowledgeable about will easily make you an influencer (opinion maker, opinion shaper or opinion leader). Influencers are going to be increasingly relied upon by buyers to shape their purchase decision.

Affiliate marketing is going to take a greater share of online marketing as the era of ad blockers make PPC (pay per click) advertising to continue becoming irrelevant.

What do you need to do?

- **Visualize** – there are billions of dollars being made by online businesses. Each of these online businesses are looking for you so that you can be a shareholder of their income (not capital!). Think of Amazon. Affiliate marketing is worth over £1 billion in UK alone. In US, affiliate marketing industry is anticipated to hit almost $7 billion in 2017.

- **Dream** – Dream of taking a significant pie of this huge multi-billion dollar industry. How much would it be if you just took 0.1% of this pie? That would be not less than $1 million. With this industry continuing to grow at an average compounded rate of about 10% per year, this is a great investment to make. Your dream of big undisrupted passive income streams can become a reality. All you need is to actualize your dream.

- **Actualize** – For a dream to come true, you have to wake up. Start working. Join an affiliate program, look out for products to market, create a blog, start marketing and become an active and passive income earner. A share of this multibillion dollar pie is definitely yours for the taking.

Deciding on your product niche

Deciding on your product niche is one of the most important decisions that you need to make pertaining to your affiliate marketing endeavor.

For more information on deciding on your product niche, please read the section on "How to Find Products to Market".

Setting up a niche website/blog

As an affiliate marketer, you are, in essence, a publisher. Thus, you need to be able to easily manage your content. Your website/blog should be capable of enabling you to publish, pend, schedule, modify, trash or delete content. A blog is a special website with Content Management System (CMS) that enables you to carry out all these functions.

For more information on setting up a niche website/blog, see the section on "Using Your Blog to Market your Products".

Finding the best Affiliate Merchant/Platform

Your affiliate network platform is extremely important to your success as an affiliate marketer. This is important since the measurement of your performance and income is determined by your affiliate platform.

For more information on finding the best Affiliate Platform, see section on "Which are the Best Affiliate Marketing Platforms?"

Getting affiliate links

Once you enroll with an affiliate network, you will be provided with affiliate links depending on the products that you choose to promote.

For more information on getting affiliate links, please read the section on "Which are the Best Affiliate Programs?"

Cloak your affiliate link

Link cloaking simply refers to beautifying an ugly link so that it can become easy to scan and much easier to master. It also involves safeguarding your link against hacking. Most affiliate links are 'ugly' because they have username information, product information and affiliate id. These make it a huge chunk of information that is unfriendly to human reading and human memory. The riskiest part of them is that they expose your Affiliate ID. Ingenious criminal hackers can easily replace your Affiliate ID with their Affiliate ID thus redirecting the reward of your effort to their own account. Hence, while link cloaking beautifies the link, it also secures your Affiliate ID by concealing it from prying eyes. One of the most popular link cloaking software for affiliate links is ThirstyAffiliates.

Sample of cloaked links

Prior to cloaking;

http://www.vendor.com/products/?product_id=111&affiliate=11 1

After cloaking;

http://www.sharewits.net/refer/productname

The benefits of link cloaking

- Stopping theft of your commission – With link cloaking, unscrupulous marketers cannot use malware to fetch your Affiliate ID and replace with theirs on the link thus redirecting your effort to their own accounts. When they redirect record of the click action to their own accounts, they earn commission that belonged to you since it is recorded on their account and not your own.

- Increased CTR (Click-Through Rate) – Cloaking beautifies an otherwise ugly link making it attractive to readers. This makes them more likely to click on the link or even share it out.

- Increased email delivery rates – Most email servers have spam detectors that easily redirect emails with affiliate links to spam box. When an email enters spam box instead of the inbox, it is very difficult for one to even tell that an email was sent or delivered. Cloaking your affiliate link make spam detectors consider your link as non-spam which makes it get delivered to the inbox.

- Improved tracking – most cloaking plugins have metric system where clicks on your links are tracked. This helps you determine which posts, pages or part of your blog generate most successful traffic (have the highest conversion rate)

- Easy to make no-follow links – Search engines, especially Google, abhor following affiliate marketing links. They feel like they have been tricked into enabling free adverts. Thus, when they discover such, they are more likely to punish you by lowering your index ranking or even not ranking you at all. To avoid this, you have to put a 'no-follow' attribute to your affiliate link. This informs search engines not to follow your affiliate link while indexing. This helps you safeguard yourself from being punished. It is hard to do this manually when links are many or when you don't have programming skills. However, with the help of link cloaking apps, this is done on the fly.

- Evade ad-blockers – Ad-blockers have become common these days. They have greatly damped ad marketing since they are increasingly being installed by users to block ads from appearing on pages while reading. Ad blockers use certain algorithm that detect ads and affiliate links. When you cloak your link, they cannot detect the affiliate element on it thus allowing ads to go through.

- Easy management of links – when you have a niche blog where you have links from several affiliate marketing networks, it becomes more laborious to manage all of them. Link cloaking plugins have provisions that allow you to easily manage various links from one central place.

Write blogs relevant to your product

As an affiliate, you are in the business of publishing. You are publishing content and leveraging it with affiliate links. Thus, the first and foremost thing is your content and then your affiliate ads.

The ads must be relevant to your content if you intend to optimize on the impact of your content on your affiliate marketing.

For more information on writing blogs, please read section on "Using Your Blog to Market Your Products".

Create a landing page

A landing page is core to your affiliate marketing campaign. It is where you make a call-to-action effort to convert your audience into potential customers.

For more information on creating a landing page, please visit section on "Using Your Blog to Market Your Product".

Device appropriate marketing strategy

It is important, once your blog is up and running, to device marketing strategy to propel your affiliate marketing effort so that you can optimize on returns.

The following are appropriate elements of your marketing strategy

- Device means and ways to build audience and retain loyal following

- Device means and ways to boost traffic flow to your site

- Device means and ways to increase conversion rate

- Device means and ways to optimize your income flows

We shall be discussing all these strategies from this point forward.

Use email marketing to drive traffic

Email marketing is still one of the most dominant online marketing tools. It is an extremely effective affiliate marketing tool if well utilized.

For more information on how to use email marketing to drive traffic, please read section on "Using Email Marketing to Market Products".

Automate your Affiliate Marketing Income

What distinguishes a small-scale affiliate marketer from a super-affiliate marketer is the degree by which automation is carried out. Of course, the easiest way to begin as an affiliate marketer is to start off as a solopreneur. But, you must scale-up to grow. Otherwise, you will remain dwarfed and overtaken by immense opportunities available to those who have mastered the art of automation.

To learn more on how to automate your affiliate income, please visit section on "How to Automate Your Affiliate Marketing Income".

WHICH ARE THE BEST AFFILATE MARKETING PLATFORMS?

Affiliate marketing platforms are the most preferred option for both the product merchants and affiliate marketers. This is because they are well equipped and positioned to match buyers of affiliate marketing service (product merchants) and suppliers of affiliate marketing service (affiliate marketers). Thus, they are marketplaces for both product merchants and affiliate marketers to meet, interact and transact.

Not all affiliate marketing platforms are the same. Thus, you need to establish criteria that will enable you to find the best affiliate marketing platform for you. This is very critical for the success of your affiliate marketing endeavor.

Criteria for choosing the best affiliate marketing platform;

1. Reputation
2. Commission percentage
3. Range of products to market
4. Diversity of income streams
5. Payment terms

6. Terms of service

Reputation

Reputation is the first and foremost criterion for choosing your Affiliate marketing platform. Reputation is built based on integrity and positive customer experience. The integrity of your affiliate marketing platform is critical in determining how much you are earning. An affiliate marketing platform that lacks integrity is more likely going to shortchange you on your income. You definitely don't want to sweat for nothing. You don't want to lose on the reward of your effort. Reputation is paramount.

Commission percentage

Different affiliate marketing platforms charge different commission rates on the same product. This is just the normal way you would expect the same product to be priced differently by different retailers. The commission percentage is often negotiated between the product merchant and the affiliate merchant. Thus, depending on the performance and reputation of the affiliate merchant, you are likely going to be offered higher or lower commission percentage. Once you have established a list of reputable affiliate marketing platform (the top 3) you can make a commission percentage comparison to find which one offers the best commission payout.

Range of products to market

An affiliate marketing platform is first and foremost a marketing place. You obviously would like to go to a market that has a wide variety of products. This increases your chances of getting the product that you want. In this regard, you should seek an affiliate marketing platform that has a wide variety of products to market. This will more likely result in more products available within your chosen niche. This enriches your blogging endeavor as you can easily optimize revenue streams from your content as you too offer a variety of products for your audience to choose from.

Diversity of income streams

Diversity of income streams largely depends on:

- The range of products being offered by a particular affiliate marketing platform – the wider the range of products offered, the more likely you are going to have more products to market within your respective niche.

- The range of affiliate ads being offered per particular product. Some affiliate marketing platforms only offer in-text links. Some others offer text plus animated links, while others add video links to the already mentioned options. The wider the options the easier it is for you to optimize your content and affiliate links. Each of these types of affiliate ads count as an income stream as probably a client who would not have clicked on an in-text link would probably click on either a video ad or an animated flash ad.

Payment terms

The ability to transform your affiliate earning into cash is of utmost importance. Some affiliate marketing platforms have limitations on how you cash out your income. Some strictly insist on direct bank transfer to a local bank within the platform's jurisdiction (e.g. US bank only). Some offer check payment method in addition to direct bank transfer. There are others who are flexible enough to offer email-based payment methods such as PayPal and Skrill.

Apart from your ability to convert your affiliate earnings into cash, you need to know how often you can withdraw your earnings and the minimum amount that you can withdraw. Most affiliate marketing platforms have a set minimum amount that you can withdraw ranging from $20 to $100. Yet, some have limitations on the frequency as some can only allow you to withdraw every once a week or twice a month, etc. Check on the payment terms to avoid earning what you cannot enjoy.

Terms of service

Terms of service are critical to your choice of affiliate marketing platform. You have to keenly read on finer details. Don't overlook any detail. Some affiliate marketing platforms are unforgiving when you violate on certain terms. This may lead to huge penalties or even outright suspension of your account. Thus, read on terms of service before committing yourself to a particular affiliate marketing platform.

The best known affiliate marketing platforms

Over time, there are certain marketing platforms that have won resilience and progress to become the platforms of choice for most product merchants and affiliate marketers.

The following are the top 5 affiliate marketing platforms that you can choose from as a starting point as you continue to evaluate each based on the kind of niche you are focused on;

- Commission junction

- Clickbank

- ShareAsale

- Linkshare

- <u>Amazon Associates</u>

Unlike others, Amazon Associates focuses only on products sold on Amazon marketplace. Thus, it is more of a merchant-driven affiliate platform. It is the most preferred affiliate platform if you are marketing products already on Amazon platform. However, if you are not marketing products already on Amazon platform, then, you will have to consider the first four platforms.

Middle Insert for Paperback

A Short message from the Author:

Hey, are you enjoying the book? I'd love to hear your thoughts!

Many readers do not know how hard reviews are to come by, and how much they help an author.

I would be incredibly thankful if you could take just 60 seconds to write a brief review on Amazon, even if it's just a few sentences!

Please head to the product page, and leave a review as shown below.

Customer Reviews

☆☆☆☆☆ 2

5.0 out of 5 stars ▾

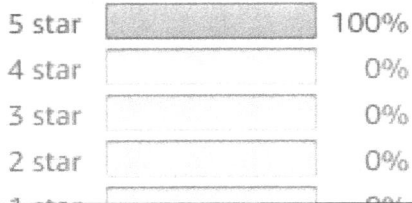

5 star	[████████]	100%
4 star	[ ]	0%
3 star	[ ]	0%
2 star	[ ]	0%

Share your thoughts with othe

Write a customer review

Thank you for taking the time to share your thoughts!

Your review will genuinely make a difference for me and help gain exposure for my work.

End insert for paperback:

The end... almost!

Reviews are not easy to come by.

As an independent author with a tiny marketing budget, I rely on readers, like you, to leave a short review on Amazon.

Even if it's just a sentence or two!

So if you enjoyed the book, please head to the product page, and leave a review as shown below.

Customer Reviews

⭐⭐⭐⭐⭐ 2

5.0 out of 5 stars ▾

5 star	████████████	100%
4 star		0%
3 star		0%
2 star		0%

Share your thoughts with other customer

Write a customer review

I am very appreciative for your review as it truly makes a difference. Thank you from the bottom of my heart for purchasing this book and reading it to the end.

HOW TO FIND PRODUCTS TO MARKET

Without a product, there is no market. Without a product, you are not a marketer. Thus, finding products to market is an important endeavor that will determine how far you succeed in your affiliate marketing endeavor.

Criteria for choosing your niche product

The following criteria will help you decide on the most appropriate product niche;

- **Choose a product niche that aligns with your passion** – Blogging is about passion. Thus, you have to choose a product niche that aligns with your passion so that you match with your content. As an affiliate marketer, you are a publisher. Trying to publish content that doesn't align with your passion will cause you to tire sooner than later. Passion is what drives you and that which will make you to continue writing against all odds. Affiliate marketing is not a sprint race but a marathon race. The focus is on long-term gains rather than short-term gains.

Many give up quite too soon because they were disappointed that the product that they were trying to market didn't pick up as soon as they expected. This won't be the case if you are blogging for passion as your income is simply a fringe benefit.

- **Choose a product niche that is available on your preferred network platform** – Not all network platforms are the same. There are those that are reputable and match your needs and there are those that do not. Once you have decided on your best platform, check the range of products offered and if your product niche falls in. If it does, that is great, if not, find the next best alternative to your preferred platform or product niche.

- **Choose a product that is profitable** – Profitability of a product is determined by first, the commission offered (both in terms of rate and amount), how fast the product is likely to turnover (the frequency of sales per given period e.g. per month) and your minimum expected rate of return (Return on your investment e.g. hosting cost and publishing costs). Different product merchants have different rates of commission. Yet, different network platforms offer different rate of commission on the same product. Thus, while you decide on the most profitable product carry out research to find the best commission rate among the best platforms.

- **Choose a product that you can continue marketing in the long-term** – Seasonal and one-off products are not ideal for your affiliate marketing if you are just beginning to establish yourself as they dry out for long. If you want your affiliate marketing endeavor to be an investment, choose products that are going to continue having consistent demand for several years to come. This way, you can publish evergreen content, that is, content that remains relevant for many years to come. You will continue earning from continued promotion of your affiliate links due to this content for as long as the product still remains in the market and the affiliate link remains valid.

Steps to choosing your niche product

Once you have established appropriate criteria, you can now venture into the actual search for your ideal product. You can choose one of the best affiliate marketing platforms as your choice for niche research e.g. CJ, Clickbank, ShareAsale, Amazon Affiliate, etc. For purposes of our demonstration, we can choose

Clickbank for the time being. The advantage of Clickbank is that it has gravity index.

Step 1: Click on Clickbank Affiliate Marketplace to get list of categories as unveiled below

MARKETPLACE

Choose from thousands of great products t

Resources

Bookmarks

Recently Removed

Categories

- ▸ ARTS & ENTERTAINMENT
- ▸ BETTING SYSTEMS
- ▸ BUSINESS / INVESTING
- ▸ COMPUTERS / INTERNET
- ▸ COOKING, FOOD & WINE
- ▸ E-BUSINESS & E-MARKETING
- ▸ EDUCATION
- ▸ EMPLOYMENT & JOBS
- ▸ FICTION
- ▸ GAMES
- ▸ GREEN PRODUCTS
- ▸ HEALTH & FITNESS
- ▸ HOME & GARDEN
- ▸ LANGUAGES
- ▸ MOBILE
- ▸ PARENTING & FAMILIES
- ▸ POLITICS / CURRENT EVENTS

How t

1. Bro

2. Use
to sea

To vie
click t
how n
sales.
HopL

To lea
Marke

New t

The C
help y

- •

- •

- •

49

Step 2: Click on a category that you are passionate writing about so that you can get its subcategories. In this case, we can click on Health and Fitness category.

This unveils the following subcategories;

We choose Diet and Weight Loss as the most preferred subcategory. Once we click on this subcategory, the following outcome unveils;

Displaying results 1-10

Re

Health & Fitness : Diets & Weight Loss

butes

Sort results by:
Popularity

100+

Fat Diminisher Is A Conversion Monster! $10,000 Prize In January! (view mobile)
Top CB Affiliates Are All Switching To This New Health Offer & Conversions Are

This shows that there are 396 products falling onto 40 pages.

Step 3: Filter out products based on Gravity index

We have to refine this list further by using gravity index (of 6) as our measure of product performance. This yields the following results;

Advertisement

Results

Resources

Bookmarks

Recently Removed

Displaying resu

Health & Fitness : Diets & Weight Loss

Reset Filters and Attributes

Filters

Sort results
Popularity

Gravity

6   100+

Fat Diminisher Is A Conversion Monster! $10,000 Prize In January! (view mobile)
Top CB Affiliates Are All Switching To This New Health Offer & Conversions Are

As can be seen, the list of items that meets gravity 6 and above has come to 63 items down from the previous 396 items.

At this stage, we can go through the displayed items to find the ones that fit into our most appropriate niche (target audience).

Step 4: scan through the items to see whether they can lead to some notable keywords as clues for further research.

Looking at the above results keenly, we can see "red smoothie detox". This is obviously a secondary keyword. We need not narrow ourselves to the extreme as our niche will be limited. Thus, we can choose the primary keyword from "red smoothie detox". This primary keyword is "detox".

Step 4: Refine the search further by using appropriate keyword (e.g. "detox")

We know that 'diet and weight loss' is a secondary keyword and there is bound to be high competition for this keyword. We can experiment with keywords associated with both diet and weight loss to find the best of them. For example, we can type 'detox' to see how the list narrows down. This brings out the following outcome;

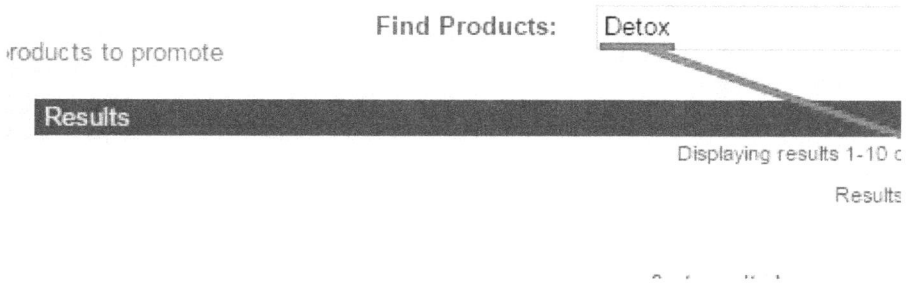

Find Products: Detox

roducts to promote

Results

Displaying results 1-10 c

Results

Using the keyword 'Detox' on the search bar, it yields 23 products. This is fine enough to scrutinize each item in detail.

Step 5: Carry out deep analysis of the keyword on search engines (e.g. Google)

There are two important Google tools that you can use to carry out analysis of the keyword

- Google Keyword Planner

- Google Trends

Google Keyword Planner

Google Keyword Planner helps you to establish how competitive the keyword is. That is, how frequently people are searching using the keyword. This is an indicator of demand for products associated with the keyword. The advantage of Google Keyword Planner is that it also provides statistics of secondary keywords and long-tail keywords associated with your keyword research. You can also create your own long-tail keywords from idea generated from the various secondary keywords and still use this keyword planner to determine their competition.

Another advantage of Keyword Planner is that you can easily use information provided to come up with a domain name for your niche blog. You too can use information provided by the Keyword Planner to carry out marketing campaign. That is, creating content around the keywords and also advertising using the keywords in your CPA (Click per Action) campaigns to drive traffic to your blog.

Google Trends

Google Trends help you to determine the long-term trend of your desired niche. To succeed in generating long-term income streams from your marketing endeavor, you need niche with a stable and relatively rising long-term trend. This will assure you of an evergreen niche.

USING EMAIL MARKETING

Emailing has proven over time that it still remains a potent tool for online marketing. This is because many people still consider emails as the best hub of communications from various sources. That's why over 200 billion emails are sent every day.

In marketing, you need to be able to generate leads. Leads are potential contacts that could result into sales.

For email marketing to succeed, you need to compile a list of emails of potential customers. Sources of email contacts include;

- General directories

- Professional directories

- Trade directories

- Landing pages

While there are entities that sell email lists, it is important to note that they are not always reliable. Some are obtained through unscrupulous means and could have been used in spamming campaigns. Using emails that have been targets of spamming campaigns will cause your reputation to be injured as the email owner will assume that you too are a spammer and thus block you or treat you as a spammer.

The best way to get email list is organically, that is, through request for exchange. This increases your reputation and the person who accepted your request is more likely going to respond to your email more positively.

Benefits of using email marketing

- **Permanency** - Email marketing, unlike other forms marketing such as telephone, it remains permanent. Thus, both parties can easily refer to a particular email when conversing

- **User-friendly format** – You can easily customize emails to have rich format (text, graphics, animation, videos, etc). With email marketing, you can actually send an email that comprise of your entire landing page and can appear as such in the inbox. This enhances user experience which promotes positive response. In this case, the user won't have to go back to your site but straight to the product's page for a quick purchase.

- **Mass targeting** – with emails, you can easily design one email and target a whole group of people e.g. doctors, lawyers, dentists, fitness trainers, etc. this increases your reach at a much lower cost (of one email) yet increases the likelihood of turning the potential lead into a sale.

How to use/launch email marketing

The following are the steps needed to launch email marketing campaign;

1. Gather email contacts

2. Create target groups

3. Group emails according to target groups

4. Create an email list for each of your target group

5. Configure each of these lists into your mail server

6. Formulate your message as per the target group. Each target group should have its uniquely crafted message that meets its needs and can persuade them to become customers

7. Schedule your mailing so as to have the most optimal impact e.g. taking advantage of special holidays, special events, etc. Make sure that your content is grammatically

correct, highly enriched, inspiring, persuasive and on target.

8. Release your mails to potential targets as per schedule.

9. Respond promptly to any feedback resulting from your email campaign.

Email marketing strategies

The following are some of the strategies that can easily lead to your email marketing success;

1. **Personalize your message** – Personal touch is critical to effective communication. Thus, let your message have some personal touch. Engage in first-person communication.

2. **Let your email be mobile-friendly** – It is estimated that about 58% of emails are opened on mobile phones as opposed to desktops.

3. **Segment your subscribers** – Segmenting your subscribers makes it easy to target them with custom messages.

4. **Automate email campaigns when possible** – More so, as part of the post-sale service

5. **Time your email delivery** – Studies have found out that 8:00 pm to midnight are the best times to send emails. Also, emails sent on weekends have a better response than those send on weekdays. Thus, it seems when people are free is when they are focused on their emails as they have enough time to digest the message. They are also less stressed and thus likely to respond more positively.

6. **Keep the subject line succulent** – Make the subject line rich in details yet short enough to be succinct.

7. **Reward your most loyal customers** – Those customers who have been consistently responding to your mail, you need to reward them. Free gifts can do. This will boost their following and references.

8. **Include landing page** – Yes, your email should have call-to-action segment.

USING YOUR BLOG TO MARKET YOUR PRODUCT

Most affiliate marketers use blogs to publish content and market their products. Blogs are the most widely used form of website for affiliate marketing purposes.

Why a blog?

A blog presents so many advantages over ordinary website.

Advantages of a blog over other kinds of websites;

- You can easily manage and manipulate content

- You don't need to have advanced programming skills to install, run and manage it

- Most CMS, are by default, structurally SEO friendly

- You can change content without necessarily changing the structure of your website

Types of CMS

There two main ways to categorize blogs;

- Either free or paid

- Either self-hosted or non-self hosted.

Popular CMS

There are over 50 CMS in the market today. However, the most popular CMS are;

- WordPress

- Drupal

- Blogger

WordPress has two options;

- Self-hosted – The self-hosted type of WordPress is found at wordpress.org which is available for you to download and host it yourself.

- Non-self-hosted – The non-self-hosted WordPress is found at wordpress.com and is available for you to easily subscribe and start posting

Drupal is self-hosted while blogger is non-self-hosted.

Advantages of self-hosted CMS;

- You own the content

- You can customize the blog to meet your specific needs

- You can easily switch your CMS from one host to another

Disadvantages of Self-hosted

- Requires time and skills to setup

- You have to find a host and pay for hosting

Advantages of non-self-hosted CMS

- It is ready-made. Thus, you simply need to subscribe and login to start posting content

Disadvantages of non-self-hosted

- You have no control over your most critical and most important asset – your content

- There is a limit as to how much you can customize your blog.

Why self-hosted WordPress is the best CMS for you

There is no doubt that, if you consider your content as your most important asset, then, you would naturally want to self-host. Also, you would naturally desire to spend less cost on acquiring the CMS. This rules out blogger and other non-self-hosted CMS. It also rules out non-free CMS. In this case, there are very few candidates left to compete with self-hosted WordPress CMS. Such other competitors include Drupal, Joomla, among others.

However, WordPress stands out from the crowd due to the following reasons;

- It is less bulky

- It is easy to use

- It has a large community of users

- It has the largest community of developers

- It is so easy to install

- There are plenty of plugins that can help you optimize SEO, Affiliate marketing, automate income and many others.

- There are plenty of themes to boost the 'look and feel' of your blog.

Most host providers can install WordPress for you at no extra cost. There are several specialized WordPress host providers that you can engage to help you out on this.

Top 10 features of a Great Affiliate Blog

While you are building your blog, it is important to know the top 10 features that make a great affiliate marketing blog;

1. A great first impression
2. Good header
3. Trusted brand
4. Inspiring content
5. Easy Navigation
6. Consistency
7. A Compelling Pre-Sell
8. Great Response (more so, to comments and forums)
9. There is always a reason to come back
10. Quick loading

Steps to building your blog

The following are important steps that will guide you in building your blog;

1. Determine your type of blog

2. Choose a domain name

3. Register your domain

4. Open a host account

5. Install your blog CMS

6. Create blog content

7. Promote your blog (so as to build audience and generate traffic)

8. Monetize your blog

Determine your type of site

There are several types of affiliate sites;

- Daily deals
- Price comparisons
- Product review
- "How to" sites
- General sites

Choose a domain name

Choosing your domain name is extremely important for purposes of SEO and user scanning.

The following steps will help you choose the most appropriate domain for your blog;

1. Come up with a domain name that matches your product (niche)

2. Match the domain name with seo keywords of your product/niche

3. Make the domain name as short as possible (without compromising on 1 & 2 above) – this is for easy scanning and memorization by readers
4. Choose non-limiting domain extension
5. If domain you want is taken, slightly modify it without stripping it of core essence (1 & 2 above)

Register your Domain Name

Once you have a domain name, the next thing is to register your domain. The process of registering, though extremely simple, varies from one domain registrar to the other. In case of difficulties, you can always get assisted by your domain name registrar in the setup process.

The following are popular domain registrars where you can easily register your domain;

- Namecheap

- Godaddy

Namecheap is the most preferred of the two options. Godaddy used to be the best but it has descended due to its insistence of compliance with government policies that restrict internet freedom, more so, when it comes to protecting the anonymity of domain ownership.

Open a host account

Once you have registered your domain, the next step is to host your domain account. Hosting is simply providing a space for your web content and directing your domain address to it so that the web content can be available when people enter your domain address to access it.

There are thousands of hosting service providers. However, the following are the most known;

- Hostgator

- Bluehost

- Siteground

- Scalahosting

The process of hosting varies from one host provider to another. Nonetheless, most hosting providers would be willing to guide you in setting up your website at no cost.

Install your blog CMS

Once you have successfully registered your domain and it has fully propagated (that is, the domain name is recognized by servers across the world) you can go ahead and install your WordPress blog.

Most hosts, like the ones mentioned above, have CPanel. CPanel is simply a dashboard with tools and resources that enables you to manage and optimize your website. The most popular of these tools is known as Softaculous.

Softaculous is a tool that enables you to install your WordPress blog without complications. It is automated. All you need is to fill in the required details in a form provided by it. These details include;

- Your blog name

- Your blog email address

- The folder in which you intend to install your blog (just provide the name of the folder). The folder must not be existing as Softaculous will automatically create it.

Once you provide these key details plus some other basic details, you simply need to click on the 'Install' button for Softaculous to automatically install the blog for you. Within 30 seconds, your blog will be up and running.

Select a great theme

Softaculous has a wide variety of themes which you can select prior to installing your blog (prior to clicking the 'Install' button). For a start, select an appropriate theme among those provided by Softaculous. You can later on easily change them when you find a better one that suits your content and layout.

You can find ideas on theme sources and other relevant information on WordPress from WPexplorer. Themeforest is another great place to find WordPress themes.

Create your blog content

Content is King! Yes, this is a very old but provocative adage that continues to perpetually renew its relevance day after day. When it comes to a blog, nothing is as important as your content.

How you write your content will determines whether it will lead to further positive action by your audience or not. You have hone the skills of a great copywriter to be able to inspire your audience so as to establish a loyal following. Practice makes perfect. Most of the copywriting skills are acquired through practice. Just be keen on gathering feedback from your audience and be ever willing and ever ready to respond to their inquiries and opinions. This way, you will be able to master what ticks them most.

Steps to a great affiliate marketing copy

The following are just but a few of the steps you need to create a great affiliate marketing copy;

1. Study Competitors
2. Research and Understand your customers
3. Know the action you are targeting and have goals
4. Develop your hook and how you put it into use (hook is a captivating phase in the first paragraph to pushes the reader to keep on reading, that is, get hooked on)
5. Target only one audience in your article/copy
6. Know how to answer "what's in for me?"
7. Know how to utilize the space above the fold (header) properly
8. Use captions with photos
9. Keep sentences and paragraphs short and to the point.
10. Simplify your language for easy understanding
11. Highlight and format text to make it outstanding
12. Find the single most important thing to your audience

13. Focus on your audience as opposed to your product. Your audience is buying a solution (key benefit), not a product
14. Use pre-headlines
15. Use video presentations to build credibility (especially confirming your claims/assertions)
16. Position credibility elements above the headline (e.g. certifications, accreditations, awards, etc)
17. Brainstorm multiple headlines (to find the best)
18. Make your headline easy to read and memorize
19. Question-type headlines

How to write a successful pre-sell

1. Manifest a profound understanding of the product you are marketing
2. Highlight key product benefits
3. Understand your audience
4. Focus on the audience, not the product
5. Use subtly persuasive language
6. Respond to questions
7. Create anticipation (about the likely outcome of using the product)
8. Use compelling authenticity (social proof e.g. testimonials, facts, statistics, infographics, etc)
9. Make the deal sweet

10. Use the links sparingly (don't overload your readers. Three links are sufficient [you can add many more links in the footer section as 'relevant links'])

Promote your blog

If you want to experience great impact on your affiliate marketing effort, you have to build audience. The larger the audience, the higher is the potential of your success.

To build audience, you need to;

1. Pamper your audience.

2. Direct traffic flow to your blog

Pampering your audience

The best way to pamper your audience is through freebies. Freebies don't have to be expensive. The following are some of the freebies that you can offer

- Free content

- Coupons

- Gifts

Content as freebies;

- Product Promotion Articles
- Product Reviews and Comparisons
- 'How to use' product articles

Coupons

Most merchants have coupons. Some of the Affiliate platforms allow you to customize these coupons to have personalized features. Personalized coupons are the best way to pamper your audience without them feeling that you are just giving them that which they would have otherwise received without your effort.

Gifts

Loyal audience need to be rewarded. Find gifts to award to your loyal audience. The following are simple gifts that you can award your loyal audience and customers;

- **Free samples** – If you have performed well and won the heart of a product merchant, you are likely going to get free samples to help you in your marketing endeavor. Take advantage of this to reward your loyal audience/customers.

- **Tickets to product events** – Product launch events are a great opportunity for your loyal audience to get exposure. Some product merchants would grant free tickets to such events. Ask for some to award to your loyal audience/customers.

- **Certificates** - when you have a large following, your loyal audience would definitely wish to be considered a cut above the rest in terms of loyalty. Giving them certificate of loyalty can make them feel great. It is another way of enabling them to attract more audience to your blog as they show off their certificates.

Directing traffic flow to your blog

One thing that you must not forget is that there are millions of blogs out there. Out of these millions of blogs, just less than 25% of them have ever received a visit. Don't consign yourself to the 75% of the ghost blogs. Make yours stand out. These blogs are not visited not because they are bad nor have nothing worth attention. It is simply because they haven't been discovered. People are simply not aware that they actually exist. You have to break away from this. You have to direct traffic to your blog so that people get to know that your blog actually exists. Once you direct traffic to your blog, obviously, you got to have great content to retain traffic. Yes, it doesn't serve purpose to direct huge traffic to your blog if you can't retain a significant portion of it.

The following are some of the ways by which you can direct traffic to your blog;

- Organic SEO
- Paid SEO (PPC)
- Social media PPC
- Email marketing
- Forum discussion
- Commenting on niche-related blog
- Social media profile
- Youtube video posting

Monetize your blog

Monetizing your blog is the process of making your blog earn you some revenue. Affiliate marketing is one such a way.

To monetize your blog through affiliate marketing you need to use;

- Personalized coupons
- Create internal affiliate links
- Link and banner ads of affiliate products in sidebar
- Make a call-to-action through landing pages

Landing pages

Landing pages are extremely important to your call-to-action. There are basically two main types of landing pages;

- Click-Through landing page
- Lead generation landing page

Click-Through landing pages

These are landing pages that redirect an audience to a certain specific target, e.g. a product page, shopping cart, etc.

Lead Generation landing pages

Lead generation landing pages are geared towards extracting leads from audience. The most important lead is the reader's email and reader's name. To be able to entice the reader to provide these details, the reader must clearly be answered about "what is in for me?" Yes, the reader must anticipate value gain in exchange of this information.

Some of the value items that a reader can gain include;

- Free eBook
- Newsletter subscription

- Free webinar

- How-to-Guide

- Coupons

- Free tickets

- Free product sample (remember to include shipping address requirement as part of the lead generation)

- Notifications of future offers

Secrets to a great landing page

- It must have a call-to-action campaign

- It must not distract the reader – avoid excessive distractions like navigation links, too many animations, excessive coloration, etc.

- It must have few details

- It should have minimal images

- It should have large fonts

Blogging for success

The following are important tips you need in order to blog for success;

- Engage your target audience
- Stick to your niche lane
- Be consistent (making audience continue to expect more and new. It is this expectation that will keep them coming)
- Magnetize your content and monetize its magnetism
- Make honest reviews
- Write a review in a personal tone
- Promote products that you are already using or likely to use
- Create demo videos explaining how to use the promoted product
- Always update your audience about new product launches or new product features

OTHER WAYS TO ATTRACT TRAFFIC

Apart from blogging and email marketing, there are several other ways by which you can attract traffic to your affiliate products. These include:

- Guest blogging

- Social media marketing

- Offering linked freebies such as free eBooks and free apps

Guest blogging

Guest blogging refers to registering to send posts to authority sites on topical issues that you are expert in. The primary aim of guest blogging is to have an opportunity to expose yourself and your blog and gain valuable backlinks to your blog.

Important things that you must consider before posting a guest blog;

- **Reputation of the website you are guest-blogging on** – Your reputation as a guest-blogger will highly depend on the reputation of the site you are guest-blogging on. Don't offer to guest-blog on a site that has low reputation as this will lower your very own reputation thus resulting into negative perspective by your potential audience.

- **The site's web traffic** – Your intention for guest-blogging is to enable you to get backlinks to your site. That is, redirect traffic from your guest-blog to your very own blog. The higher the traffic on the guest-blog the higher is the potential of redirecting more leads to your blog.

- **Relevance of your topic to the website** – It is important to be particularly considerate of the site's target audience. You need to know the targeted demographics, i.e. whether it is teenagers, youth, adults, male, female, general, etc. It would be irrelevant to post an article on trending fashion clothes on a technology site. This will have less impact, but if your blog is about technology, then, this will have great impact.

- **Whether the site's webmaster will allow you to place backlinks to your site** – The most important aim for you to carry out guest-blogging is to redirect potential audience to your site. Thus, backlinks matter a lot. Obviously, most webmasters will restrict the number of backlinks and the places where you will be putting the backlinks. Most allow you to place backlinks on your attribution. If the site does not allow backlinks, then, your chances of redirecting traffic are almost none. Don't bother guest-blogging on such a site.

- **Whether the site's webmaster will allow you to have an attribution to your post** - Unless the webmaster is absolutely mean, as a guest-blogger, you are entitled to put attribution to your post. If this is not allowed, simply don't guest-blog on such a site.

- **Terms and conditions provided for guest** - Blogging by the site's webmaster- check on terms and conditions relevant to guest-blogging prior to deciding on whether to guest-blog or not. Guest-blogging is a mutually beneficial relationship. If the terms and conditions serve to disadvantage you, then, simply consider not guest-blogging on such a site.

Social media marketing

The death of article directories, at least in terms of their relevance, meant that publishers had to seek alternative ways of generating backlinks to their sites. Social media marketing has emerged as one of the most powerful means of redirect traffic to your site.

The advantages of social media marketing are numerous. The following are just but a few of them;

- There are very few restriction

- There is huge volume of potential audience

- There are plenty of tools available to enable you to automate your posting to and from your blog

- You can have multiple pages each dedicated to a particular niche

- You can easily get feedback concerning your social media marketing campaign

- Your performance metrics are easily available and for free

- You can easily launch your advertising campaigns inside that particular social media (more so Facebook)

- There is a variety of social media to choose from including Facebook, Twitter, Pinterest, StumbleUpon, Tumblr, LinkedIn, among others

- There is high level of interaction with social media

The most popular social media networks

There are over 50 social media networks. The following are to most popular;

- Facebook
- Twitter
- Google plus
- Pinterest
- LinkedIn
- Instagram
- StumbleUpon
- Tumblr

How to succeed in social media marketing

To succeed in social media marketing, you need to consider the following key points;

1. Ensure brand consistency across platforms
2. Ensure content consistency (quality, quantity, relevance, timing)
3. Create inspirational statements (for lack of better word)
4. Be informative
5. Be engaging
6. Provide newsworthy content
7. Pingback

HOW TO AUTOMATE YOUR AFFILIATE MARKETING INCOME

The best way to become a successful affiliate is to automate your affiliate marketing income. This is achieved by assigning mundane tasks such as writing and posting blogs to other people (virtual assistants) and using automation tools so that you focus on idea generation and other creative endeavors.

As a publisher, the first and foremost thing that you need to automate is your content. You can achieve content automation through the following ways;

- Outsourcing content creation

- Outsourcing content marketing

It is imperative that, as you grow you will need to expand your scope by having more niches. Each niche will require its own website blog. Thus, you will need to create several websites. You can automate blog creation in the following ways;

- Outsourcing web development

- Outsourcing niche domain research

With content automation and web development automation, the capacity becomes so large such that you need to have your affiliate links strategically placed on your blogs. To achieve this you will need;

- Virtual assistants

- Virtual administrator (in case you employ several virtual assistants)

To optimize your content and blog structure for search engines, you will need an SEO expert who will assess and evaluate the performance of your blogs on various search engines and perform the necessary tweaks to achieve optimal performance.

Automating tools

There are many automation tools available that you can use to improve automation of your income. The good thing is that WordPress has many automation tools availed as plugins. Choosing WordPress as your CMS can greatly boost your automation effort.

The following are the main categories of automation tools;

- Niche search automation tools

- Content marketing automation tools

- Web development automation tools

- Social media automation tools

- Email automation tools

- SEO tools

- Traffic performance monitoring tools

Niche search automation tools

These are tools that make it easy to find profitable affiliate niches. Some of these tools include;

- Offervault

Content marketing automation tools

Content marketing automation tools are tools that enable you to easily market your content in the most optimal way. These include

1. Forum boards;

   - Quora

   - Warrior forum

2. Product videos (YouTube) – review, instructions, applications, special features, etc

   - <u>Youtube</u>

3. Landing page creation tools;

   - <u>Ubounce</u>

Web development automation tools

These are tools that enable you to automate creation of websites. There are several such tools including Wix among others. However, in this case, we focus on those that help you automate creation of WordPress blogs. These include;

- Softaculous – this is the most widely used automation tool for creating WordPress blogs. It is a free tool installed by most hosts who offer CPanel for managing your host.

Social media marketing automation tools

Social media marketing tools enables you to post content on various social networks in the most optimized way. There are many such tools. However, the most commonly used tools include;

- AddThis – this is a multi social network plug-in that allows you to post your content on your various social network accounts.

- ShareThis – this is just like AddThis. It is simply an alternative to AddThis.

Other than these general tools, each social network has its own unique tools that enable you to post directly from your website into your social network page or timeline. Such plugins include;

- Facebook share plug-in

- Twitter plug-in

- Pinterest plug-in

- StumbleUpon plug-in

- Tumblr plug-in

- LinkedIn plug-in

To get each of these plugins, access the developer section of each of these social networks right from within your account.

Email marketing automation tools

When you have hundreds of email contacts to deal with, it becomes a tough task to post to them and promptly respond to feedback. Thus, there are various auto-responders (email posting and responding tools) that are available to enable you to automate this task. The following are some of the most popular email marketing automation tools.

- Aweber

- Mailchimp

- Getresponse

SEO tools

SEO tools are important in helping you optimize your content and also monitor the performance of your keyword. The following are some of the most widely used SEO tools

- Yoast – Yoast is a WordPress plug-in that helps you to generate optimize keywords for your content.

- Google Adsense – Google Adsense has performance metric tools that go hand-in-hand with your chosen keywords. However, this works well when you have done keyword advertisement campaign with Google so that you can gauge performance of your advertised keywords.

Traffic performance monitoring tools

- <u>Google Analytics Solution</u> – Google has a lot of tools that not only help in monitoring traffic performance of your blog but also evaluate how healthy your site is SEO-wise.

- <u>Alexa</u> – Alexa is a tool that ranks website according to their traffic performance. The lower the rank the higher the performance. A site that ranks less than 1,000 is a great performing site. If you are a newcomer, having an index of less than 100,000 in a span of three months is a huge step forward.

CONCLUSION

Thank you for your decision to get this book.

I hope the proven hands-on practical information provided in this book has inspired you to take up the challenge of taking a bite out of this multi-billion dollar industry – Affiliate Marketing.

It is also my sincere hope that you have been able turn your hobby into full-time business for a great passive income through blogging and Affiliate Marketing.

Information is power. With this book, you are able to transform others by empowering them by simply sharing with them information provided in this book. Please share out large and encourage them to have a copy for their reference and great success.

Again, thank you for getting and reading this book.

Goodluck!

www.ingramcontent.com/pod-product-compliance
Lightning Source LLC
Chambersburg PA
CBHW071501210326
41597CB00018B/2648